I BELIEVE

I can be thankful and grateful every day for one thing in my life, just like Carlo and Teddy and all their friends at the ranch

Coloring and Activity Book 10

SUZANNE MONDOUX
Illustrated by Gaëtanne Mondoux

BALBOA
PRESS

A DIVISION OF HAY HOUSE

Balboa Press books may be ordered through booksellers or by contacting:

Balboa Press
A Division of Hay House
1663 Liberty Drive
Bloomington, IN 47403
www.balboapress.com
1 (877) 407-4847

Print information available on the last page.

ISBN: 978-1-9822-2271-0 (sc)
ISBN: 978-1-9822-2272-7 (e)

Balboa Press rev. date: 02/22/2019

This book belongs to

_____

I am _____ years old

Carlo and Teddy had woken up to the first snowfall of the year. The snow had come early that year. It was the week before Halloween.

They looked out the barn door at a thin blanket of white snow over the ground. The snow weighed down the bright orange, red and yellow leaves. The mountains' white tips reached up into a white sky.

It was quiet all around. The mice were curled up in the hay bales up high in the loft. They heard Carlo and Teddy rustling below. The four mice poked their heads out of the bales. They looked down at Carlo and Teddy. Carlo and Teddy were talking low. They did not want to wake the others. But the mice were already up so they crawled out from their warm beds and climbed down the wooden beam to join Carlo and Teddy.

Carlo and Teddy were looking at their map. They were reminiscing on their journey together as friends. A gentle breeze came through the barn. The map fluttered and folded here and there. The mice ran quickly to the four corners of the map to hold it down. They sat and listened to Carlo and Teddy talk about all the places they visited. But most importantly, they talked about their friendship. They were honored and most thankful to have been able to share this together. And they knew there were lots more to explore.

Paul and Suzie poked their heads into the barn. The girls and boys at the ranch had also been friends for a very long time.

Paul and Suzie, now ten years old, had come to the ranch when they were six. They walked quietly into the barn. They looked down at the map spread over the floor. The four mice waved good morning while they nibbled on their breakfast. Teddy had served them apples for breakfast.

"Come in," said Carlo. "Are Julie and Sam still sleeping?"

"They are finishing their breakfast. They will be joining us soon," said Suzie.

Before long everyone was gathered in the barn. Sparky the little black dog ran in like a tornado swirling through the barn. He was always ready to talk about everything.

Lulu the fawn Pug trotted into the barn. Her two pups Bessie and Tulip, now almost all grown up, whisked past her.

Carlo and Teddy had sent word to Cody from the beach, and Baxter the black and white Pointer mix from the playground up in the mountains overlooking the ranch, to join them for the harvest fest party on the ranch. They too joined in on the early morning discussion in the barn.

Max the orange tabby cat jumped up on the wooden beam above their heads. With his body stretched out across the beam he smiled at everyone, his new friends and family.

Jojo and Sara prepared hot cocoa for everyone. Together they sat in a circle and talked about what they had to be thankful for.

Suzie stood up and smiled at everyone. "Be as it may, life is amazing. We just have to want it to be amazing in all of our tiny amazing moments, just like sipping on a nice cup of tea, or cocoa. I am thankful for all of my tiny and big moments, especially this nice cup of hot cocoa. I believe every moment of my life is an opportunity for me to learn and grow and to enjoy. I now know I decide what meaning I chose to give to every tiny and big moment."

"Hear, Hear!" said everyone. They raised their cups.

Things to be THANKFUL for

Animals

Friendship

Kindness

Nature

Laughter

Music

Self Love

Sam, now twelve, had come to the ranch when he was eight. He tapped his feet on the ground. He jumped up on a bale of hay. "No man, no woman, no one, no industry, no country, no anything needs to dominate to succeed! Your intentions for a greater good will get you there! I am thankful to have learned to lead with a feather instead of a hammer. I believe I can lead instead of bully." He put his hands together and raised them to his heart. "I am thankful for all of you in my life." He bowed forward in gratitude.

Everyone put their hands together and brought them to their heart and bowed with Sam.

Julie was eight years old when she came to the ranch. She was now twelve. She sat on the blanket with her legs crossed. "I am thankful and grateful that I now know that my and our most precious possession is our soul. I believe one must be kind and loving and compassionate to those who hurt it. By healing those who hurt you will heal yourself as well." She wiped the tears from her eyes. Everyone did the same. They all had a tiny tear trickle down their cheek. She looked up at everyone and bowed her head. "I love you all. Thank you for helping me and helping me heal my self, for helping me heal my own soul."

Paul climbed up on the beam next to Max. He sat on the beam with his legs dangling below. "I am thankful and grateful that I have witnessed the coexistence with animals and humans here at this ranch. I believe that coexistence with animals will be the humans' greatest victory. May we have the courage to conquer our greatest fears that wait for us! Many humans do not believe this is possible. And the thought of it is what frightens them. The reason I see this being fearful for many humans is this – one of the problems, the vision, the belief humans have is that they can compare themselves to animals. We are all Beings. Animal Beings and Human Beings. Humans believe they can compare themselves to Animal Beings. They believe Animal Beings can be treated less than a Human Being! No Being – Animal or Human need to be treated with anything less than love and kindness. I suggest we see Animals for who they are, and not as a comparison to Humans. I ask that all humans stop saying 'they treat us like Animals!' All the Animal Beings, all Beings thank you for this."

Everyone looked up at Paul. They had never heard him speak as such, let alone for that long. Paul had always been a quiet boy who said very little. He spent most of his time reading and writing. Not long ago it would have taken a great deal of encouragement to get Paul to join Max up on the beam. Paul would always stay in the back on his own not wanting to be seen or known by anyone. Today he had shown courage and wisdom.

Max sat on his lap. He reached his front paws around his neck and gave him a big hug.

Everyone below stood up on their feet and clapped loudly.

"I am thankful and grateful for all of you. I am also thankful and grateful for tomorrow because I now look forward to it: the mystery of the unknown. And I will write all about it!"

Believe in Yourself

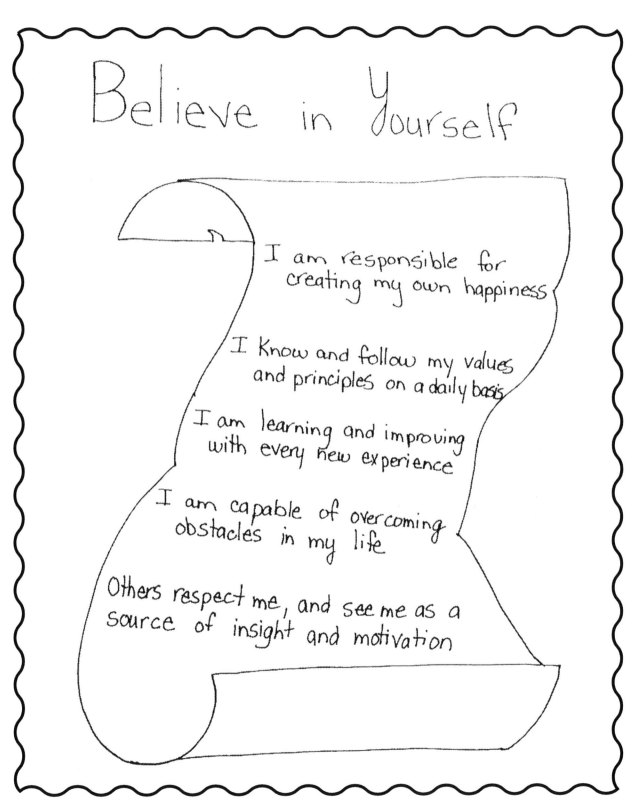

I am responsible for creating my own happiness

I know and follow my values and principles on a daily basis

I am learning and improving with every new experience

I am capable of overcoming obstacles in my life

Others respect me, and see me as a source of insight and motivation

The rest of the morning everyone was busy with preparing for the harvest fest party. By lunch time the warm autumn sun had melted the snow. The ground was dry and the sky was bright blue.

Later in the day many Animal Beings and Human Beings gradually arrived at the ranch. The Beings gathered and talked and laughed together. The festivities went on late into the night. All Beings danced and sang under the harvest moon.

The girls and boys of the ranch were so thankful and grateful that they could share with you what they were most thankful and grateful for, that they invite you to write what you are most thankful and grateful for.

For the next 60 days write once a day what you are most thankful and grateful for in your life. It can be big or small. It can be anything you want to be thankful or grateful for.

Also, write what you will do, and be thankful and grateful for that will help humans better coexist and live in harmony with animals.

Let your imagination take you anywhere it wants to take you!

Lets begin.

Most importantly - Have fun!

Remember to smile.

Remember to laugh.

Remember to be curious and ask questions.

Remember to Believe in yourself.

Say out loud 10 times.

I Believe in myself.
I Believe in myself.
I Believe in myself.
I Believe in myself.
I Believe in myself.
I Believe in myself.
I Believe in myself.
I Believe in myself.
I Believe in myself.
I Believe in myself.

Day 1

Day 2

_____

_____

_____

_____

_____

_____

_____

_____

_____

_____

_____

_____

_____

Day 3

Day 4

_____

_____

_____

_____

_____

_____

_____

_____

_____

_____

_____

_____

_____

Day 5

_____

_____

_____

_____

_____

_____

_____

_____

_____

_____

_____

_____

Day 6

_____

_____

_____

_____

_____

_____

_____

_____

_____

_____

_____

_____

Day 7

_____

_____

_____

_____

_____

_____

_____

_____

_____

_____

_____

_____

_____

Day 8

_____

_____

_____

_____

_____

_____

_____

_____

_____

_____

_____

_____

Day 9

Day 10

_____

_____

_____

_____

_____

_____

_____

_____

_____

_____

_____

_____

Day 11

Day 12

_____

_____

_____

_____

_____

_____

_____

_____

_____

_____

_____

_____

Day 13

_____

_____

_____

_____

_____

_____

_____

_____

_____

_____

_____

Day 14

Day 15

_____

_____

_____

_____

_____

_____

_____

_____

_____

_____

_____

_____

_____

Day 16

Day 17

Day 18

_____

_____

_____

_____

_____

_____

_____

_____

_____

_____

_____

_____

Day 19

Day 20

_____

_____

_____

_____

_____

_____

_____

_____

_____

_____

_____

_____

_____

_____

Day 21

Day 22

_____

_____

_____

_____

_____

_____

_____

_____

_____

_____

_____

_____

Day 23

_____

_____

_____

_____

_____

_____

_____

_____

_____

_____

_____

_____

Day 24

_____

_____

_____

_____

_____

_____

_____

_____

_____

_____

_____

_____

Day 25

Day 26

_____

_____

_____

_____

_____

_____

_____

_____

_____

_____

_____

_____

Day 27

Day 28

_____

_____

_____

_____

_____

_____

_____

_____

_____

_____

_____

_____

Day 29

_____

_____

_____

_____

_____

_____

_____

_____

_____

_____

_____

_____

Day 30

_____

_____

_____

_____

_____

_____

_____

_____

_____

_____

_____

_____

_____

Day 31

Day 32

_____

_____

_____

_____

_____

_____

_____

_____

_____

_____

_____

_____

Day 33

Day 34

Day 35

Day 36

_____

_____

_____

_____

_____

_____

_____

_____

_____

_____

_____

_____

Day 37

_____

_____

_____

_____

_____

_____

_____

_____

_____

_____

_____

_____

Day 38

_____

_____

_____

_____

_____

_____

_____

_____

_____

_____

_____

_____

Day 39

Day 40

Day 41

_____

_____

_____

_____

_____

_____

_____

_____

_____

_____

_____

_____

Day 42

_____

_____

_____

_____

_____

_____

_____

_____

_____

_____

_____

_____

Day 43

Day 44

_____

_____

_____

_____

_____

_____

_____

_____

_____

_____

_____

_____

Day 45

Day 46

Day 47

Day 48

Day 49

_____

_____

_____

_____

_____

_____

_____

_____

_____

_____

_____

_____

Day 50

_____

_____

_____

_____

_____

_____

_____

_____

_____

_____

_____

_____

Day 51

Day 52

Day 53

_____

_____

_____

_____

_____

_____

_____

_____

_____

_____

_____

_____

_____

Day 54

Day 55

_____

_____

_____

_____

_____

_____

_____

_____

_____

_____

_____

_____

_____

Day 56

_____

_____

_____

_____

_____

_____

_____

_____

_____

_____

_____

_____

Day 57

_____

_____

_____

_____

_____

_____

_____

_____

_____

_____

_____

_____

Day 58

_____

_____

_____

_____

_____

_____

_____

_____

_____

_____

_____

_____

Day 59

Day 60

WOW! YOU ARE AMAZING!!!!!!!!!!!!!!
YOU DID ALL THE FUN STUFF!

YOU PARTICPATED IN 60 DAYS OF FUN!

KEEP GOING!

EXPLORE YOUR IMAGINATION!

BELIEVE IN YOURSELF ALWAYS!

SHARE WHAT YOU ARE MOST THANKFUL AND
GRATEFUL FOR IN YOUR LIFE, AND THE EXPLORATION
OF YOUR IMAGINATION WITH A FRIEND!

THANK YOU FOR BEING GOOD AND
KIND TO EVERY ANIMAL.

On behalf of all the ANIMALS – thank you for
making this a better world for ALL OF US!

Printed in the United States
By Bookmasters